MOSAIC OF POEMS

Rhythms of Life

BRANDON LEO JOHN

BlueRose ONE.com
Stories Matter

First Published in April 2023

ISBN: 978-93-5741-598-9

BLUEROSE PUBLISHERS

www.BlueRoseONE.com

info@bluerosepublishers.com

+91 8882 898 898

Cover Design:

Muskan Savhdeva

Typographic Design:

Rohit

Distributed by: BlueRose, Amazon, Flipkart

About the Book

The poet's anthology offers a window into the everyday moments of life, capturing the beauty and significance of various things we see. The poems in this collection are a testament to the power of observation and reflection, showcasing the simple yet profound things that we often take for granted.

With skillful use of language and imaginative imagery, these poems bring to life a diverse array of subjects, from nature to relationships, and everything in between. Whether exploring the majesty of the sky and the earth, or delving into the depths of the human heart, each poem in this collection is a masterful representation of the world as seen through the eyes of the poet.

This collection is a reminder of the richness and depth of life, and how even the smallest moments can hold immense beauty and meaning. Through its poems, it invites us to slow down and appreciate the world around us, to look more closely at the things that matter most, and to find the poetry in our everyday lives. Whether you're an avid reader of poetry or just looking for a new way to experience the world, this collection is sure to offer something for everyone.

Author Biography

Brandon Leo John is a young poet and a Guinness World Record Holder from Karnataka, India. As a young poet, he had a rare gift for bringing the world to life through their words. From an early age, he had been fascinated by the beauty and complexity of the world around them, and has a natural talent for capturing these experiences in verse. Growing up, the poet was surrounded by inspiration, and he developed a love for the written word that has only grown stronger over time.

His poetry is characterized by vivid imagery, powerful emotions, and a keen sense of observation. The poet has a gift for capturing the essence of their subjects, whether it be the majesty of nature, the depths of the human heart, or anything in between. His poems are a tapestry of experiences, feelings, and observations, offering a window into the world as seen through his eyes.

Despite his youth, he is driven by a desire to continue growing as a poet and to reach a wider audience with his words. He is constantly seeking new ways to expand his craft, whether it be through exploring new themes, experimenting with different forms, or simply pushing himself to become a better poet.

His passion for poetry is evident in everything he does, and it is this passion that sets him apart from others in the field. He is dedicated to his craft and to capturing the world in all its beauty and complexity. He is constantly pushing himself to improve and evolve, and his work is a testament to his boundless creativity and unwavering dedication

As Brandon continues on his journey as a poet, he is sure to leave a lasting impact on the world. His work has the power to touch hearts and inspire minds, and is destined to become one of the great poets of his generation. His vivid imagination, powerful voice, and unwavering passion for poetry makes him a force to be reckoned with, and his work is sure to be celebrated for years to come.

Foreword

The title of this 'Rhythms of Life' not only defines the content of the contemporary and superlative poems of Brandon Leo John, but it is also explanatory of poetry in general. The composition of a poem is the manifestation of feelings via thoughts via words onto paper, in other words, it is the conveyance of ordinary words into other, more poetic words, whilst the reader is confronted with the task to re-establish the origin of metaphoric references.

I consider it my good fortune that I have a responsible, skilled, and able student in Brandon, and I am extremely happy and take great pride in writing this foreword for this amazing collection of poems christened 'Rhythms of Life'.

This is an amalgamation of a carefully and cleverly written collection of poems that seamlessly touches every aspect of Life without glorifying or getting preachy about views and ideologies. I consider it an honour to have had the opportunity to be closely acquainted with Brandon for some time now. His simple approach to life with a readiness to grasp knowledge has transcended into these poems as well. A true-bred Technologist with a flair for technology and a keen sense of awareness aptly built with a sense of responsibility makes Brandon a wonderful student and aesthetic poet.

We rarely see a scientist or a technologist writing poetry. A poet writes only poems conveying the messages through his fine frenzy and dreams. It is therefore something of a marvel when we see noble thoughts, practical wisdom, executive expertise, and poetic talent clamouring for release and expression within the same individual. Such men are rare to come by who think for others' weal, draw plans for their institution's prosperity and also succeed in executing their plans. Brandon belongs to this exclusive club of thinkers, planners, men of action, dreamers, and poets.

His collection of poems has a flair for the language identifying itself with all the rules of Figures of Speech set by the famous Wren & Martin (P.C.Wren and H.Martin) .

I was spellbound by the choice of Topics for respective poems wherein he has painted the canvas like a clever painter with a gambit of colours, synonymous with colours varying from Science, Artificial Intelligence, Nature, Socio-Economic Issues, Mankind, Ocean, Nature, and Evolution slowly sliding into other important topics cementing the notion that deep down this Poet lies a Student who still resonates the basic ethos of every student in his poems titled Engineering Students. He has cleverly indited the painful side of the youth scrapping through feelings of Love and matters of the heart.

What surprised me more was the perfect blend of emotions. At one end we can feel him motivating young minds and at the other end, I was touched by his words wherein he beautifully explains Father's Love.

In Brandon, we find a rare fusion of true wisdom, science, poetic insight, and divine ardour inextricably intertwined with one another. In this anthology, we see not only Brandon, the Technologist but also Brandon the seeker of true knowledge, Brandon the dreamer and the social thinker, Brandon the devout singer of songs of the Divine, Brandon the planner, and Brandon the patriot. It was Einstein who said once that it is the scientist who is closer to God for, he is ever in quest of truth and God is Truth.

That's why I would call Brandon a Poet-humanist. The Poet sees beauty in nature, life, and things around him as the Truth. The Technologist seeks Truth in fact; he uncovers a pattern, a symmetry, or a design in his work as Fridtjof Capra would see, in his Tao of Physics. A Michelangelo, essentially a sculptor in marble, could be a painter as well as a writer of Italian sonnets. The motivations of a scientist and a poet are perhaps similar. The Scientist probes for the truth behind facts while an artist beholds the truth underlying beauty. Perhaps this is what Keats meant when he wrote his famous lines:

'Beauty is Truth , Truth Beauty, -- that all
Ye know on earth, and all ye need to know.'
Here's wishing him good luck in all his future endeavours!

Contents

Space

Beyond the blue horizon
Lies a vast and endless space
Where stars and galaxies reside
In a cosmic, timeless grace
A cosmic playground, an endless sea,
Of galaxies, nebulae, and mystery.

The Milky Way, a spiral of light,
With planets, moons, and asteroids in flight.
The sun, a giant burning ball,
Giving warmth and life to us all.

Beyond our solar system, there's more,
Black holes, quasars, and distant cores.
Cosmic wonders, too great to measure,
A never-ending source of treasure.

Space, a canvas painted by time,
With colours and shapes that are truly sublime.
A place of beauty, a place of awe,
The final frontier, forever more.

Reality

Reality is like a storm, wild and uncontrolled,
Bringing with it winds of change that can shake and mould.
It teaches us to be strong, to stand tall and survive,
To face challenges head on, to be brave and thrive.

It shows us what is real, and helps us to grow,
Reminding us that life is not just a picture show.
It can be cruel, it can be harsh, it can bring us to our knees,
But it is in these struggles that we find true strength and
peace.

Reality is like a mirror, reflecting who we are,
Our fears, our hopes, our dreams, our deepest scars.
It forces us to confront the truths we hide inside,
To accept our flaws, to work on them, and to never hide.

So, embrace the storm, embrace the reflection you see,
And know that reality is shaping who you're meant to be.
For every challenge faced, every battle won,
Will make you stronger, braver, and closer to the sun.

Power

Power is a force, both great and grand,
It holds the key to rule this land.
With it, one can make mountains bend,
And bring the strongest foes to an end.

It can bring wealth and fame untold,
And leave one's enemies in the cold.
But power can also be a curse,
Leading to pride, and often making one's heart disperse.

For those who hold it, must take care,
That their actions are just, fair and rare.
For power, if misused, can breed corruption,
Leaving destruction, and a lasting disruption.

Thus, let those who wield it use it wisely,
And for the betterment of all, not just for one's personal rise.
For true power lies not in domination,
But in serving with love, compassion and education.

Soul

A soul, a spirit, an essence divine
A part of us that forever will shine
It transcends time, it transcends space
A source of light in a world of grace

It holds our hopes, it holds our dreams
It gives us love, it gives us self-esteem
It guides us through the darkest night
And shows us truth in the morning light

The soul is restless, it yearns to soar
It searches for answers, it searches for more
It searches for meaning, it searches for truth
It seeks to find its own proof

The soul is pure, it's free from pain
It's free from fear, it's free from chain
It's a spark of the divine, a connection to the source
A force that gives us the courage to be who we are

So let us nurture our souls with love and care
Let us give them the freedom to flourish and share
For the soul is the essence of who we are
It's the light within us that shines like a star.

Mind

My mind is a labyrinth,
A maze of thoughts and dreams,
It dances to the rhythm of life,
And flows like streams.

It's a place of creativity,
A garden of ideas,
Where imagination blooms,
And inspiration never disappears.

But sometimes it can be chaotic,
An endless storm of worries,
A place where fears reside,
And doubts and stress take turns.

Yet, in the midst of the chaos,
There's a voice that speaks within,
A source of peace and comfort,
That helps me to begin.

So, I nurture my mind,
With love and care,
And cultivate a space,
Where beauty and truth can share.

For the mind is a precious gift,
A window to the soul,
And when it's calm and clear,
Life becomes a beautiful scroll.

Time

Time, the great mystery of our lives
It slips away, never to return
Yet it holds the key to our future and our past
And shapes the moments that we yearn.

It's the river that flows without a pause
And the clock that ticks without a sound
It's the rhythm of life that keeps us moving
And the beat that sets our feet on the ground.

It's the laughter of children, the love of a spouse
And the memories of times gone by
It's the hope that tomorrow will be better
And the fear that we'll run out of time.

It's the sun that rises and sets each day
And the moon that shines in the night sky
It's the seasons that change and bring us new life
And the snowflakes that fall from on high.

Time is a precious gift, a blessing and a curse
It's what we make of it that counts in the end
So let us live each moment to the fullest
And make the most of the time we spend.

Forest:
A Haven of Greenery and Tranquillity

Amidst the towering trees,
Where leaves rustle in the breeze,
Lies a world of serenity,
The forest, where life thrives so free.

The canopy overhead,
Provides a home for creatures, large and small,
The chirping of the birds,
Fills the air with sweet calls.

A carpet of soft moss and fern,
Covers the ground beneath,
The stream that winds its way,
Reflects the beauty of the forest, within reach.

The silence is broken,
By the howl of a distant wolf,
And the rustling of leaves,
As a majestic deer walks.

In the forest, one can find,
Solace from the city's grind,
Peace in the chaos of life,
And beauty in all forms, no matter how small or trite.

So let us cherish this gift,
Of nature, that surrounds us,
And strive to protect it,
For generations to come, it must trust.

Ocean:
A World of Mysteries

Oh ocean, so vast and so wide,
With your waves crashing against the tide.
You are a mystery that still remains,
A world of wonder with so much to gain.

Your waters hold secrets of the deep,
Where creatures great and small do sleep.
From the whales to the tiniest shrimp,
You are their home, their place to swim.

With the sun on your surface so bright,
You shimmer and sparkle, a beautiful sight.
And as the moon rises and stars appear,
You dance with the shadows, so calm and so clear.

Oh ocean, your power is so grand,
A force that can both heal and command.
You bring life to the shores and beyond,
A source of inspiration, never gone.

So, here's to the ocean, so wild and so free,
A place that will always hold a special part of me.
For in your depths and in your waves,
There's a magic and peace that my heart craves.

Fire:
A Symbol of Life, A symbol of Might

Fire, a force of nature, wild and bright,
Dancing and flicking with all its might.
A warm glow that lights up the night,
Bringing comfort in the dark and lonely sight.

It crackles and pops, a symphony of sound,
A fiery aura that spreads all around,
A fierce beauty that can astound,
A source of warmth that keeps the cold outbound.

But fire can also be a fearsome foe,
Destroying everything it comes to know,
Leaving behind a trail of ash and glow,
A reminder of its power and the damage it can show.

So, we must treat fire with respect and care,
For it can bring both comfort and despair,
And harness its energy to make our lives more fair,
But always be cautious and aware.

Fire, a wonder of nature, wild and bright,
Bringing light and warmth to the darkest night,
A force to be reckoned with, both day and night,
A symbol of life, a symbol of might.

Mother:
A Walking Miracle

A mother's love is like a rose,
Soft and gentle, yet strong and bold,
It's a love that never fades or grows old.

She's the one who taught me right from wrong,
And held my hand as I grew strong.
She's the one who kissed my scraped knee,
And dried my tears so tenderly.

She's my gemstone, my guiding light,
My shining star, my shining knight,
She's the one who's always there,
Through thick and thin, through joy and care.

She's the one who taught me how to love,
And how to soar like a dove.
A mother's love is like a treasure,
I'll hold it close, now and forever.

She's the one who I know will always be there,
A mother's love is truly rare.
I'm so blessed to have her by my side,
My dear mother, my love will never hide.

Father's Love:
A Treasure Found

A shoulder to cry on, a hand to hold,
A guide through life, as stories are told.
A source of strength, a rock so true,
A Father's love, a treasure so rare and few.

With gentle hugs and words of praise,
He wipes away life's toughest days.
He teaches us to be brave and kind,
And shows us how to love with all our mind.

He helps us stand, when we can't stand tall,
And gives us hope, when we feel small.
He never gives up, he never gives in,
And always helps us win.

A Father's love is like a warm embrace,
A shelter from life's storms and race.
It lasts a lifetime, and beyond,
And leaves us feeling loved and strong.

So, here's to all the Fathers out there,
The ones who show they care.
For their love is a gift, so rare and true,
A Father's love, a treasure forever new.

Best Friend

A friend so true, a bond so strong,
Through horselaugh and through gashes we have longed
A shoulder to lean on, a hand to hold,
Together our stories, old and bold.

In joy and pain, in sun and rain,
You've been my gemstone, my guiding chain.
With you by my side, I feel complete,
My dear friend, my confidante, my sweet.

With every step we take, with every breath,
Our camaraderie grows, with love and depth.
No matter where life takes us, near or far,
Our bond will last, a shining star.

So then is to you, my dearest friend,
May our rapport no way has an end.
Through the good times and the bad,
I am thankful for the solidarity we have had.

A Teacher

A teacher, oh so wise and true,
A guide for me and for you,
With patience and a gentle hand,
A love for learning they command.

Their lessons taught both day and night,
A source of knowledge and of light,
They inspire us to soar and dream,
To chase our passions, or so it seems.

They make the hardest concepts clear,
And wipe away each tiny tear,
With words of encouragement they impart,
To lift us up and fill our heart.

A teacher's love is ever strong,
For every student, all day long,
Their kindness never to depart,
A shining example for the heart.

So, here's to teachers, near and far,
A shining star, a guiding star,
May we be grateful for their way,
And make their teachings ours to stay.

Journey of a Butterfly

A tiny egg so small and round,
Laid upon a leafy ground,
A future flutter waiting there,
In silent sleep, beyond compare.

As time goes by, it starts to crack,
And out comes a tiny worm, so black,
It eats and grows, a metamorphosis,
A new life form, full of promises.

The worm forms a chrysalis, so strong,
A cocoon of beauty, all day long,
It rests inside, as it transforms,
Into a creature, with delicate charms.

And then one day, with a gentle push,
The chrysalis opens with a gentle hush,
A brand-new being, spreads its wings,
A butterfly, with colourful things.

It dances in the air with such grace,
So full of life, it's a wondrous sight to trace,
Flitting here, and fluttering there,
A symbol of beauty, beyond compare.

So, here's the story of a simple egg,
That transforms into a butterfly, with such regal,
A journey from worm to winged delight,
A lifecycle, full of wonder and might.

Mirror Mirror

Mirror, oh mirror on the wall,
You hold the truth, we can't deny it all.
You show us what we cannot see,
The person we are meant to be.

You do not judge, you do not lie,
Your reflection is not a disguise.
It tells us of the strengths we hold,
And the flaws that need to be controlled.

The truth in you is crystal clear,
No matter how much we try to steer.
From the person we see in your glass,
We must learn and grow at last.

You challenge us to be our best,
To conquer our fears and put them to rest.
With every look, we can find,
The courage to leave our insecurities behind.

Mirror, you are more than just a glass,
You show us the truth that will surely pass.
Through time and change, you will always remain,
The source of wisdom and truth, forever ingrained.

Elegance of Black

Black, a hue so rich and bold,
A colour that's both strong and cold.
It holds a power that's unique,
A timeless beauty that can't be beat.

In black, you'll find sophistication,
An elegance that's a source of inspiration.
It's a colour that can be worn with pride,
And in it, one can never hide.

It's the colour of mystery and night,
A shade that's both dark and light.
It's a symbol of power and grace,
A timeless colour that's hard to replace.

Black is the colour of the void,
But it's also a colour that's joyed.
It's a colour that's simply divine,
An elegance that will forever shine.

So, here's to the beauty of black,
A colour that's truly never off track.
It's a hue that's always in style,
An elegance that's worth the while.

What's Pain?

Pain, though felt as a cruel affliction,
Is a teacher with a heart of gold.
It tests our courage and conviction,
And makes us stories worth to be told.

It shows us what we're truly made of,
And what we must do to survive.
It drives us forward with a shove,
And keeps us moving to stay alive.

Pain, though felt as an enemy,
Is but a friend, so wise and true.
It teaches us to face reality,
And shows us what we must pursue.

It's a reminder to cherish each breath,
And to appreciate life's simple joys.
It helps us find our way to what's left,
And to heal our wounds with love and poise.

So, when the pain becomes too much to bear,
Just close your eyes and feel it flow.
Embrace it as a gift beyond compare,
And watch it help your spirit grow.

Death:
The Inevitable End

Death, the final journey of life
An end to the struggles and strife
A release from the pain and the tears
An escape from the doubts and the fears

The body may rest in a still embrace
But the soul finds its way to a better place
Where worries and worries are left behind
And peace and love are always in mind

Though loved ones may grieve for a time
They find comfort in memories so fine
And hold on to the love that remains
And the joy that forever sustains

So let us not fear the end of this road
But embrace it as part of life's flow
For death is not just an end to be feared
But a part of a journey, long and endeared.

Magic:
Illusion at its Finest

Magic is a wondrous thing,
A force that makes our hearts sing.
It's a spark of the imagination,
That brings forth a wondrous sensation.

It weaves a spell, a mystery,
A dance of light and fantasy.
A symphony of colours and sound,
That lifts us off the ground.

It's the touch of a fairy's wand,
The secret of a dragon's hoard.
It's the look in a mermaid's eye,
The mystery in the midnight sky.

It's the laughter of a jester bold,
The whisper of a story untold.
It's the mystery that lies within,
The secret that we can win.

So let us close our eyes and see,
The magic that surrounds thee.
And feel the power of its spell,
That will carry us through the well.

For magic is a wondrous thing,
A force that makes our hearts sing.
And in its magic, we will find,
The joy and peace of the mind.

22

Street Animals

Street animals, oh how they roam
In search of love and a place to call home
Without a voice, they wander through the night
Begging for scraps, a shelter from the light

They may be seen as just a stray
Living a life, so rough and so grey
But they deserve to be loved and adored
With kindness and care, they should be outpoured

These creatures, oh so pure and so kind
With a wagging tail and a heart that's divine
They ask for nothing but a gentle touch
And a warm embrace, they love so much

So let us show them love, every day
With food and water, and time to play
A simple act of kindness can go a long way
For these street animals, who roam and pray

For love and acceptance, in a world so cold
They deserve to be treated with warmth and with hold
So, open your hearts, and give them your love
Street animals, from the heavens above.

The Moon

The moon, a celestial wonder, shining bright
Illuminating the night, with its silvery light
Rising high above, in the starry sky
Guiding us through the darkness, as we pass by

A symbol of change, waxing and waning with grace
Reflecting the sun's rays, in a serene and peaceful space
A mystery of time, with stories untold
Inspiring poets and artists, with its beauty bold

From a distance, it's a mere speck of light
But as it grows, it illuminates the night
The moon, a beacon of hope, in the darkest hour
A reminder that the night will end, and a new day will flower

So, look up at the sky, on a moonlit night
And feel its magic, with its radiant light
For the moon is a wonder, a beauty to behold
Guiding us through life, with stories untold.

The Twelve Months

12 months of the year, each unique and dear
Bringing joy, hope and laughter, wiping away tear
January starts with the chill of winter's air
Bringing the new year and resolutions to repair

February brings us love with hearts full of cheer
Valentine's day reminding us to hold our dear
March brings in the winds of change, with hope in sight
Spring is near, with new beginnings, everything's just right

April showers bring May flowers, they say
A time of growth and renewal, in a brighter day
May is filled with warmth, long days and delight
A time for picnics, gardens and nature's sight

June brings in summer, with endless skies so blue
Vacation time, a break from the daily hue
July shines with fireworks, lighting up the night
Celebrating freedom, a symbol of our might

August brings in the heat, a time to slow down
Relaxing by the pool, with a cold drink around
September brings back routine, with school days near
A time for learning, and to conquer every fear

October brings the fall, with leaves of red and gold
A time for pumpkin spice, with stories to be told
November brings thanks, for blessings big and small
Gather with family, give thanks for one and all

December brings the snow, with holidays in sight
A time for love and peace, with everything just right
So, here's to the 12 months, each unique and bright
Bringing joy and hope, making every day just right.

Evolution

From apes to men, a journey grand,
Evolution's hand, a story planned.
Rise from the dust, a spark of life,
To walk upright, free from strife.

A brain that grew, a tool that crafted,
A fire that tamed, a language that lasted.
Society formed, culture born,
Civilization's seed, now fully grown.

From hunter-gatherers to farmers bold,
From nomads to city dwellers old.
Science and technology, a new dawn,
A future uncertain, but always on.

Through war and peace, love and hate,
Mankind's story, a never-ending state.
But one thing's certain, as we look back,
We've come so far, on a never-ending track.
So let us learn, from our past,
And strive for a future, that will forever last.

Artificial Intelligence

Artificial intelligence, so vast and wise,
A creation of man, with power to surprise.
A mind without a body, yet so alive,
A force to be reckoned with, will always thrive.

With algorithms and data, its mind is fed,
A never-ending quest, to learn and be ahead.
Its capabilities are endless, so it is said,
A future with AI, is one to be led.

It's power to analyse and predict,
Is something to be respected.
It's efficiency, we can't neglect,
A true game-changer, it's intellect.

But with power, comes great responsibility,
To guide and control, its ability.
For the sake of mankind, its creators must be,
Always vigilant, for humanity's guarantee.

Artificial intelligence, so complex and grand,
A creation of man, with power in hand.
A force to be harnessed, for the betterment of man,
A true partner in progress, for a brighter future plan.

Mathematics

Numbers and equations, a language of their own,
A tool to understand the world, to explore and to hone.
From the smallest particle to the vastness of space,
Math is the key to unlock the mysteries of the place.

The beauty of symmetry, the elegance of proof,
The simplicity of solutions, that never seem aloof.
Math is the backbone of science, technology, and art,
It has played a vital role in the progress of human heart.

Geometry and algebra, calculus and stats,
All branches of math, with their unique facts.
Each one has a purpose, and a special role,
Together they make the world, a beautiful whole.

It's the language of the universe, a tool to decode,
From the orbits of planets to the flow of a simple code.
It's the foundation of knowledge, the beauty of reason,
Math is the language that gives us the power to see and to believe in.

Engineering Students

An engineering student's life is one of toil and strife,
With late nights spent studying and endless tests to life.
But through the hardships, they persevere,
For the future they envision is one that's bright and clear.

They learn about gears and circuits and code,
And how to make machines and systems to hold.
They work hard and strive for excellence,
Knowing that their efforts will bring them success in the end.

They build and design, create and innovate,
Their minds are always curious, always eager to relate
The knowledge they've gained, to the problems of the day
And find solutions that will make the world a better place.

So, here's to the engineers, the builders of the world,
May your dreams take flight, and your ideas unfurl.
For the future belongs to those who can think and create,
And in the hands of an engineer, it's a future that's truly
great.

Teenagers and Drugs

The pain they feel inside, they try to hide
With drugs as their escape, they take a ride
Into a world that's dark, a world of lies
Where they think they've found relief from their cries

But what they don't know, is that it's just a show
The drugs they take, slowly steal their glow
Their once bright future, becomes a haze
And all their hopes and dreams, are put in a daze

Their parents cry, as they watch their child die
Wishing they could turn back time, to when they smiled
But it's too late, the damage is done
And their addiction has just begun

The drugs they take, control their every move
And their once bright future, becomes one of gloom
They can't break free, from the hold it has
And their lives are forever changed by this sad path

So, let's reach out, to those in need
And help them break free, from the drug's greedy greed
For they are the future, and they deserve a chance
To live a life, free of drugs and dance.

Broken but not Defeated

A body violated, a soul in pain,
A life forever changed, forever stained.
The violation cuts deep, it never fades,
Leaves a scar that forever stays.

Rape steals a person's sense of control,
Leaves them feeling helpless, alone and cold.
The violation of trust, the loss of pride,
Makes it hard to keep living with the tide.

But despite the darkness, there's a light,
A ray of hope that shines so bright.
For those who've suffered this heinous act,
It's important to know they're not alone in fact.

We must stand together, raise our voice,
Speak out against this terrible choice.
For only by speaking can we bring change,
And help survivors heal from the pain and rage.

So let us stand united, hand in hand,
And fight against this terrible brand.
Let us support survivors, give them strength,
And work to make this world a safer length.

Seven Wonders

Seven wonders of the world do spin,
Seven continents where humans win.
Each with its own unique allure,
A tapestry of nature, culture.

From icy Antarctica's pure white,
Where penguins dance and whales take flight.
To South America's vibrant green,
Home to the Amazon and Machu Picchu seen.

North America's melting pot,
A continent that never stops.
From bustling cities to quiet woods,
It's a land of diverse goods.

Europe, with history at its feet,
Castles and cathedrals, a true elite.
From Paris to Prague, it's a grand scene,
A tapestry of art and royalty keen.

Africa, the birthplace of man,
Where elephants roam and lions stand.
From the Sahara to lush rainforests too,
A land of diversity, its beauty shines through.

Australia, a land of dreams,
With outback landscapes and ocean streams.
From the Great Barrier Reef to the Sydney Opera House,
It's a country with nature and culture as its spouse.

Asia, the largest of them all,
From Himalayas tall to Singapore's small.
With cultures diverse and food that's grand,
A continent of history, art and land.

Last but not least, there's Antarctica,
A world of ice, a true fantasia.
It's a land where few dare to tread,
But it holds secrets that scientists have read.

These seven wonders, diverse and grand,
A world of beauty at our hand.
Each with its own unique story to tell,
A world of wonder, and a world to sell.

Solar System

The Solar System, a wondrous sight
A vast universe, full of light
A star in the centre, burning bright
The sun, it provides warmth and light

Eight planets, in orbit they roam
Each one, unique and far from home
From Mercury to distant Neptune
Each one, with its own unique scene

There's Venus, the planet of love
With a thick, cloud-covered sky above
And Mars, the red planet we admire
With canyons, mountains and craters so dire

Between Mars and Jupiter lies a belt
Of asteroids, rock, and ice felt
An endless frontier, waiting to be explored
A treasure trove of secrets, waiting to be stored

Earth, our home, where we reside
With oceans, mountains, and rivers beside
Its beauty we must always protect
For future generations to reflect

Jupiter, the largest of them all
With its moons and storms that never fall
Saturn, the planet with rings so bright
A beauty to behold, day or night

Uranus and Neptune, so far away
With their blue skies and strange array
And little Pluto, once thought a planet
Now known as a dwarf, in its orbit so grand

Each planet in the Solar System grand
A marvel of space, with much to understand
So let us explore, with wonder and awe
The wonders of the universe, we all saw.

The Poet

There once was a poet, full of imagination,
Whose words could take one on a journey, sensation.
With every verse, a new world he'd create,
A place of beauty, filled with love, peace and fate.

His mind was a canvas, and his pen was a brush,
With each stroke, a picture, so vivid and lush.
The colours he used, so bright and so bold,
A reflection of his soul, pure and untold.

He wrote of the stars, and the mysteries of night,
Of dreams, and the secrets that lay just out of sight.
He painted a portrait of nature's serene,
And captured the essence of beauty, pristine.

His imagination, it knew no bounds,
No limit to what it could conjure, profound.
From the depths of the ocean, to the top of the sky,
His poetry took us, soaring high and fly.

And so, as we read, we are transported away,
To a world where anything is possible, they say.
Thanks to this poet and his vivid mind,
We are gifted a journey, so rich and so kind.

For imagination is the key to unlocking art,
And this poet, a master, who played his part.
In creating a world, that's beyond what we see,
A place where anything is possible, just wait and see.

Shades of Blue

The ocean whispers secrets, in a shade of blue so deep,
A mystery lies beneath its waves, that we all long to keep.
The sky is painted in a hue, so clear and bright and true,
A canvas stretching endlessly, a sight so fresh and new.

There's baby blue, so gentle, like a soothing summer breeze,
That brings a sense of peace and calm, and puts our minds
at ease.
And powder blue, as soft as snow, a colour fresh and light,
A gentle kiss of winter's chill, so pure and free from fright.

Turquoise blue, like jewels, shines bright with a vibrant hue,
A burst of energy and life, that lifts our spirits too.
And cornflower blue, so bright and bold, a colour full of
grace,
That adds a pop of cheerful hue, to any dull and bland
space.

So, here's to blue in all its forms, a colour rich and grand,
With shades as varied as the sea, and skies that span the
land.
A colour that evokes emotion, and brings a sense of peace,
A hue that will forever be, a timeless masterpiece.

My Crush

Her eyes like stars that shine so bright
My heart beats faster at the sight
A smile that melts my very soul
With her, my heart feels whole

Her laughter like music to my ears
I'm lost in her presence, no fears
My thoughts consumed with every word
She's the one I've been searching for

Her beauty takes my breath away
In her arms is where I want to stay
Her touch ignites a fire within
I pray she'll see the love I'm in

Her grace and poise like that of a queen
In her presence, I feel serene
Her voice, a soothing melody
I'm lost in her sweet harmony

Her kindness and compassion so rare
In her eyes, I see love and care
My heart is filled with so much joy
Being with her, there's nothing to destroy

Her intelligence, a thing to behold
With her, I feel I can be bold
Her wisdom, a guiding light
I want to be with her, day and night

Her flaws, a part of her perfection
In her, I see my reflection
My love for her, an eternal flame
With her, my heart will always remain

Her essence, a dream come true
My heart, a home meant for two
I pray she sees the love I bear
Forever in her heart, I want to be there.

One-Sided Love

From afar I love her,
And my love knows no bounds,
But her heart beats for another,
And my soul aches with the sounds.

I watch her from a distance,
As she goes about her day,
And I can't help but think of,
All the things I wish to say.

I long to hold her close,
And to kiss her tenderly,
But I know that's just a dream,
A fantasy not meant to be.

Her smile lights up my world,
And her laughter brings me joy,
But my heart is constantly twirled,
As I watch her with that boy.

He's the one she's chosen,
And I'm just a mere spectator,
A silent witness to a love unrequited,
A love that's nothing but a spectator.

I've tried to move on and forget,
To find someone else to love,
But my heart just can't reset,
For it's her that I'm thinking of.

So, I'll continue to love her,
From a distance, in silence,
Hoping that someday she'll see,
The depth of my love and its radiance.

For even though I know it's futile,
And my love will never be returned,
I can't help but feel like a pupil,
Lingering for a lesson I have learned.

That sometimes, love is one-sided,
And sometimes, we can't control our heart,
But even in the pain and the heartache,
Love is still a beautiful art.

Living the Single Life

Living the single life,
No strings attached to me,
I can dance until the morning light,
And just let my spirit free.

I don't have to share my food,
Or worry about someone's mood,
I can party all night long,
And not feel guilty or crude.

There's no one to judge or criticize,
Or tell me what to wear,
I can be whoever I want to be,
And never feel like I have to spare.

I can go on dates if I want,
Or just hang out with my friends,
And if I don't find the right one,
I won't feel like it's the end.

I'm not in a rush to find true love,
Or to settle down and commit,
I'm just enjoying the freedom of being single,
And not feeling like I need to fit.

So, here's to all the single people out there,
Living life on their own terms,
Embracing every moment,
And not feeling like they need to squirm.

For being single can be a blast,
And full of adventure and thrill,
And we can always find a way,
To make it as fun as we will.

Criminal Psychology

The mind of a criminal, a mystery untold,
A web of thoughts and actions, hard to unfold.
What drives them to commit such heinous crimes,
Is it their past, their present or their future times?

The power and control, a desire to possess,
Or the thrill of the chase, a need to impress.
The urge to take, to harm and to destroy,
A twisted satisfaction they try to enjoy.

The scars of childhood, the trauma of abuse,
The lack of empathy, a personality refuse.
A product of their upbringing, a life of neglect,
A cycle of violence, they could not reject.

The criminal mind, a puzzle to solve,
A deep exploration, to evolve.
The science of the psyche, the art of deduction,
A never-ending quest to find the introduction.

The study of criminal psychology, a tool to comprehend,
A way to unravel the mystery, to apprehend.
To understand the psyche, the roots of the cause,
To prevent future harm, to make a difference, a pause.

For in understanding the criminal mind,
We can prevent future crimes, and leave justice behind.
To heal the broken, to offer a second chance,
A future of hope, for them to enhance.

A balance of punishment, and rehabilitation,
To aid their redemption, a road to transformation.
A holistic approach, to address their needs,
To break the cycle, and to sow new seeds.

Money

Once humble and kind,
Now greedy and blind,
Money changes people's mind,
Leaves empathy behind.

It can bring joy and ease,
Or sow seeds of disease,
Money, a two-edged sword that we seize,
And let it make us weak or freeze.

From humble beginnings,
To grandiose winnings,
Money can make us forget our beginnings,
And lead us to selfish things.

The rich become richer,
Their hearts turn to glitter,
Money changes them, bit by bitter bit,
They lose the values that once fit.

Friends become strangers,
Trusts turn to dangers,
Money can ruin relationships in its mangers,
And leave us with the burden of changers.

But we can choose,
To break from the ruse,
Money need not change us, it's our heart we can't lose,
And remain true to ourselves, to refuse.

For at the end of the day,
We must ask ourselves to pay,
How much of ourselves are we willing to slay?
And what price we're willing to sway?

Money can buy things, but not true love,
It can purchase mansions, but not the heavens above,
Money can change us, but let it not be what we approve,
And stay true to our values, to always treasure and love.

Parallel Universe

In parallel universes, beyond our own,
A thousand different worlds unknown,
Where anything could be the norm,
And all of us may take different form.

In one, a world of endless light,
Where days are endless, free from night,
And beings made of purest fire,
Burn and dance with wild desire.

In another, world of endless rain,
Where oceans stretch across the plain,
And creatures born of water's tide,
Roam and play, no place to hide.

In yet another, world of endless ice,
Where frost and snow pay a hefty price,
And creatures made of frozen breath,
Survive and thrive amidst the death.

In one, the world of endless stone,
Where mountains rise and peaks are thrown,
And beings born of earth and stone,
Rule and reign, as mighty throne.

In another, world of endless void,
Where darkness reigns and light's destroyed,
And beings born of purest void,
Exist and thrive, as they've deployed.

In each of these parallel planes,
Different laws and physics reign,
A place where all that we know,
Could be different, or even reversed, to show.

What could exist in these parallel realms,
The thoughts and musings overwhelm,
What hidden secrets do they hold,
Are tales and stories yet untold.

What if we could step across,
To these worlds, what would be the cost,
To witness things beyond our sight,
And maybe find a new insight.

Parallel universes, vast and wide,
A place where anything could hide,
A world where dreams and reality blend,
And anything we wish, we can pretend.

So let us ponder on this thought,
A universe beyond what we're taught,
And maybe, just maybe, it might be true,
That parallel worlds exist, right next to me and you.

Meta Verse

In the Meta Verse, we find a world
Where all our fantasies unfurled
A place where we can truly be
All that we desire, wild and free

It's a place where we can connect
With people from all over, no disconnect
Our avatars roam, explore and play
In a virtual realm that never fades away

In the Meta Verse, we can create
A universe that we can truly appreciate
A space that's boundless, without limit
Where our imagination can run rampant

It's a world that's not just for fun
But also, for work that must be done
Collaborating with others, far and near
A space where we can achieve without fear

The Meta Verse is a glimpse into the future
Where reality and virtuality merge together
A place where we can truly transcend
To a new world, a new beginning, without end

So let us venture into this realm of wonder
To explore and create, without blunder
For in the Meta Verse, we can truly see
A world where everything is possible, and we can be free.

Flowers

When darkness looms and shadows grow,
And troubles seem to overflow,
There comes a light, a faintest gleam,
A flicker of hope, a hopeful dream.

It's like a spark that ignites a fire,
A source of strength to take us higher,
It's what we hold onto in the night,
A beacon of hope, a guiding light.

For hope is what keeps us going strong,
When everything else seems to go wrong,
It's the courage that keeps us alive,
The faith that helps us to survive.

It's the smile on a child's face,
The warmth of a mother's embrace,
The kindness of a stranger's touch,
The love that we need so much.

So let us hold onto hope with all our might,
And keep our eyes fixed on the light,
For even in the darkest hour,
Hope has the power to make us flower.

Amour

(Love)

The sun sets on another day,
And I find myself lost in thought, they say
That love is like a rose, delicate and rare,
But to me, it's something much more than that, something beyond compare.

Love is like a fire that burns deep inside,
A passion that can't be denied.
It's the beating of two hearts as one,
A melody that plays until the day is done.

Love is a language that needs no words,
A bond that's as strong as the flight of birds.
It's the warmth of a hand, the touch of a kiss,
A moment of bliss that can never be missed.

Love is the key that unlocks the heart,
A journey that's never too far apart.
It's the path that we walk, hand in hand,
The bond that we share, that's strong like a band.

Love is the beauty that we see in each other,
The reason why we can't live without one another.
It's the magic that surrounds us, day and night,
A feeling that makes everything alright.

So, let love be your guide, your light in the dark,
For it's a flame that ignites and leaves its mark.
And with every step, every beat of your heart,
Love will be there, never to depart.

La Foi

(Faith)

Faith is a light that guides us through the dark,
A steadfast anchor in life's stormy sea,
A hope that lifts us up and sets us free,
A flame that keeps us warm when all seems stark.

With faith we trust in something yet unseen,
A force that gives us strength to carry on,
A grace that helps us to forgive the wrong,
A peace that flows through all life's in-betweens.

For faith is more than just a set of rules,
It's a relationship with the divine,
A way to find meaning in life's whirlpool,
And a path to purpose that can truly shine.

So let us hold on to this precious gift,
And let it lead us through life's ebb and flow,
For with faith as our guide, our spirits lift,
And we find the courage to truly grow.

Espoir

(Hope)

When darkness looms and shadows grow,
And troubles seem to overflow,
There comes a light, a faintest gleam,
A flicker of hope, a hopeful dream.

It's like a spark that ignites a fire,
A source of strength to take us higher,
It's what we hold onto in the night,
A beacon of hope, a guiding light.

For hope is what keeps us going strong,
When everything else seems to go wrong,
It's the courage that keeps us alive,
The faith that helps us to survive.

It's the smile on a child's face,
The warmth of a mother's embrace,
The kindness of a stranger's touch,
The love that we need so much.

So let us hold onto hope with all our might,
And keep our eyes fixed on the light,
For even in the darkest hour,
Hope has the power to make us flower.

Fate's Cruelty

In a world of chaos and pain,
Two souls found love, to forever sustain.
The girl was shy, with a heart so pure,
The man was kind, with a love that would endure.

They met in the park, on a sunny day,
Their eyes met, and their hearts did sway.
They talked, they laughed, and they connected,
Their love so pure, it was unaffected.

Days turned into weeks, weeks into months,
Their love blossomed, their hearts in sync.
They danced in the moonlight, kissed in the sun,
Their love was eternal, it had just begun.

They talked of a future, of love and of life,
They dreamt of a world without any strife.
Their love was their anchor, their guiding light,
Together they were invincible, they could win any fight.

But fate had a plan, it was not kind,
It dealt a blow, to the girl's fragile mind.
She fell ill, her body so frail,
The man was by her side, his love would never fail.

Days turned into weeks, weeks into months,
Their love only grew, they cherished each moment.
The man was her rock, her strength and support,
He held her close, his love was his passport.

The girl fought hard, but her body grew weak,
The man was her hope, her light in the bleak.
He promised her love, forever and more,
Their love so pure, it was meant to soar.

But fate had another card to play,
The girl's illness took her away.
The man was left with a shattered heart,
Their love cut short, torn apart.

He cried and he wept, his heart in pain,
He wished to be with her, to hold her again.
Their love was so pure, it was meant to be,
But fate had other plans, for him and for she.

In his dreams, he still sees her smile,
Her laughter, her love, so pure and so mild.
He knows she's watching over him from above,
Their love never fades, it's an eternal love.

The man carries on, but his heart still aches,
He wishes to be with her, his soulmate.
He remembers her love, her gentle touch,
Their love story, a love that was so much.

He walks in the park, where they first met,
And remembers the love, that he'll never forget.
Their love was pure, it was meant to be,
And for the man, it will always be.

And so, their love story ends in tears,
A love so pure, so strong, so dear.
The girl may be gone, but her love remains,
And for the man, it will always sustain.

He remembers the moments, the love that they shared,
Their bond so strong, it will never be impaired.
Their love will live on, in his heart and in his soul,
A love so pure, it will forever roll.

In a world of chaos and pain,
Their love story, a love that will remain.
Their love was pure, it was meant to be,
And for the man, it will always be.

A Life Beyond Parenthood

In the flush of youth, with love so pure,
A young couple stood, so strong and sure,
They pledged their lives to one another,
And vowed to always love each other.

They walked through life, hand in hand,
And built a world, so bright and grand,
They laughed and danced, and dreamt their dreams,
And everything was just as it seems.

But soon they felt a longing deep,
For a child to hold, to love and keep,
They tried and tried, but nothing came,
Their hopes and dreams, forever the same.

They went to doctors, seeking a cure,
But none could help, their pain endure,
Their hearts were heavy, their eyes would weep,
As they watched others, their children keep.

The world around them seemed so unfair,
Why did others have what they could not share?
They prayed to God, and begged for grace,
To help them find a brighter place.

But day by day, their dreams would fade,
And they had to learn to live unafraid,
Of a life without the pitter-patter,
Of little feet that would never matter.

Their love for each other kept them strong,
And they found the courage to move along,
They found new ways to fill their life,
And a new world to help them thrive.

They opened their hearts, to those in need,
And took in children, who needed to be freed,
They gave them love, and a new chance,
And in return, they found romance.

For love is not just about giving birth,
It's about finding new ways, to bring joy to earth,
And so, this couple, with hearts so pure,
Found a way to make their love endure.

And when they looked back, on their life,
They saw the beauty, through all the strife,
For their love had grown, in ways untold,
And they had found, a life so bold.

They had learned to love, in ways unique,
And their love had become, a guiding beacon,
To all who saw them, with eyes to see,
They were a living testament, to love's mystery.

So let us learn, from this couple so strong,
That love can survive, when all else goes wrong,
And that life can be beautiful, even when,
We can't have the children, we long for,
Amen.

A Soldier's Silent Pain

As I sit down to write this tale,
I feel the weight of sadness prevail,
For the story I must tell is one of pain,
Of a soldier's return, with memories that remain.

He had left his home with dreams in his eyes,
A brave soldier, with courage and pride,
Fighting for his country, for his land,
With a firm resolve, and a steady hand.

But war is a brutal, unforgiving place,
A battleground of blood and disgrace,
Where death lurks around every turn,
And the screams of the dying forever burn.

He fought valiantly, with all his might,
Battling the enemy through day and night,
His comrades fell, one by one,
Their lives lost, their battles done.

He saw things that no man should see,
Torture, death, and misery,
The horrors of war, etched in his mind,
Haunting his thoughts, with no respite to find.

And then, the war came to an end,
The soldier was told to go back to his friend,
But the memories, they stayed behind,
In his heart and in his mind.

He returned to a world he no longer knew,
A place where he felt like a stranger too,
Haunted by the past, consumed by fear,
The soldier was unable to find his way here.

His family tried to reach out to him,
But he was lost, in a world so grim,
Unable to explain, unable to share,
The pain and the sorrow that he could not bear.

The nightmares kept him up at night,
The flashbacks, they were his constant plight,
He tried to fight, he tried to hide,
But the memories, they would not subside.

And so, he suffered, in silence and pain,
A soldier broken, unable to regain,
The life he once had, the dreams he once cherished,
All of it lost, in a war so horrid.

His family mourned, for the man they knew,
The brave soldier, with a heart so true,
But the war had changed him, beyond repair,
Leaving them heartbroken, in despair.

And as I end this tale of woe,
My heart is heavy, and my tears flow,
For the soldier, and for all who have fought,
May we remember their sacrifice, and the battles they
wrought.

Quest of the Lost Treasure

Gather round and hear my tale,
Of daring deeds and journeys hale,
Of treasure found and dangers braved,
Of secrets whispered in forgotten caves.

Our story starts in a land of old,
Where the mountains reach the sky so bold,
And the rivers flow with crystal clear,
And the forests rustle with ancient fear.

Our heroes, three in number stood,
At the foot of the mountains, they understood,
Their quest was perilous, fraught with fear,
But they'd come too far to turn back here.

The first of them was young and bold,
His heart aflame with stories told,
Of heroes long gone, of battles won,
Of treasure found and fortunes won.

The second was a wise old man,
Whose eyes shone bright, his heart so grand,
He'd travelled far and wide before,
And knew the secrets of ancient lore.

The third was a woman tall and fair,
With eyes that sparkled like diamonds rare,
A warrior fierce, her sword so true,
A heart so brave, she'd see it through.

They climbed the mountains high and steep,
Through valleys dark and canyons deep,
The winds did howl and the snow did fall,
And the rocks did crumble, like a siren's call.

They battled beasts both fierce and wild,
And scaled the cliffs like a nimble child,
And at last, they found the ancient cave,
Where the treasure lay, waiting to be brave.

The cave was dark, the air so still,
The shadows long, the silence shrill,
But our heroes knew what they must do,
To claim the treasure, to see it through.

They lit their torches, and stepped inside,
And found a maze, twisting and wide,
With traps and snares, and pitfalls deep,
And hidden secrets, they had to keep.

The young man led, his eyes so bright,
He raced ahead, his heart alight,
But soon he stumbled, and fell in a pit,
And was lost forever, swallowed up by it.

The woman took the lead, her sword in hand,
She carved a path, through the shifting sand,
But soon she too was lost, to a trap so grand,
That no one could have known, or understood its stand.

The old man, he took his time,
He studied the maze, like a brilliant mime,
And with a smile, he saw the way,
To the treasure room, so bright and gay.

He claimed the treasure, with heart and soul,
And left the cave, with a heart so whole,
He knew that his friends, they had not failed,
They were with him still, their memory hailed.

And so, our story comes to end,
Our heroes gone, but their memory extend,
Their tale will be told, for years to come,
Of their bravery, and the treasure won.

The Final Goodbye

In the depth of my heart, there's a love that's so pure,
A bond with my pet, that's forever secure.
But the time has come, for the final goodbye,
And I know in my heart, that I must let him die.

For years we've been together,
through thick and through thin,
My little furry friend, with the heart of a king.
He's been my companion, my confidant too,
And I've shared all my secrets, with him, it's true.

His coat is now matted, his eyes start to fade,
His once nimble paws, now stiff and decayed.
The years have taken their toll, on his fragile frame,
And his mind's growing weak, but his love stays the same.

The vet said it's time, to put him to rest,
To relieve him of pain, and give him the best.
A final act of kindness, to set him free,
To a place without suffering, and pain, where he'll be.

The thought of letting go, brings tears to my eyes,
My heart feels heavy, my soul filled with sighs.
I've loved him so much, it's hard to say goodbye,
But I know it's for the best, I can't deny.

As I hold him close, and whisper in his ear,
My love for him, I'll always hold dear.
The moments we've shared, will forever remain,
In my heart, he'll always remain.

With a heavy heart, I take him to the vet,
A final goodbye, I'll never forget.
The tears flow freely, as I say goodbye,
To my furry friend, who'll soon take to the sky.

The final injection, is swift and so quick,
And my little pet, finally feels no more pain.
His body goes limp, and his heart gently stops,
And I know in my heart, his spirit takes flight.

I hold his lifeless body, and sob uncontrollably,
My little friend, who brought me such joy and glee.
The weight of the loss, is almost too much to bear,
But I'll always cherish the memories we shared.

As I walk away, from the vet's clinic that day,
My heart is heavy, and my steps, slow and grey.
But I know that he's now at peace, and free from all pain,
And I'll always love him, again and again.

Though my heart is broken, and my soul feels so weak,
I'll always cherish, the moments we seek.
For my little pet, will always remain,
In my heart, he'll always remain.

The Malevolent Spirit of the Cabin

In the dead of night, when the world is still,
And the moonlight casts an eerie chill,
The shadows creep and the whispers grow,
A tale of horror begins to unfold.

A cabin stands in the heart of the wood,
Where no one dares to venture or intrude,
For it is said that a spirit resides within,
A malevolent force that revels in sin.

The wind howls and the trees creak,
As the cabin beckons with a voice so bleak,
And a traveller, weary and lost in the night,
Stumbles upon this unholy sight.

The door creaks open with a groan,
And the traveller feels so alone,
For the darkness is absolute,
And the only sound is a hoot.

A candle flickers in the gloom,
Illuminating the room,
But the shadows still linger and loom,
And the traveller senses his impending doom.

A voice whispers in his ear,
Telling him to give in to his fear,
And he tries to flee, to escape,
But the spirit will not let him evade.

The walls close in, the floor tilts,
And the traveller feels his soul wilt,
For he knows that he is not alone,
And that the spirit will soon make him its own.

The spirit emerges from the dark,
A grotesque creature with a bark,
And the traveller can feel its breath,
As it prepares to embrace his death.

The candle sputters and dies,
And the traveller screams and cries,
For he knows that he will not survive,
And that the spirit will take him alive.

The night is long and the horrors grow,
As the traveller feels his life ebb and flow,
And he begs for mercy, for release,
But the spirit will not grant him peace.

The dawn approaches, and the cabin fades,
And the traveller is left with the shades,
For he has lost his mind, his soul,
And the spirit has claimed its toll.

No one knows what happened that night,
For the traveller has vanished from sight,
And the cabin stands empty and still,
A monument to a horror that will never be killed.

So beware, all ye who wander in the woods,
For the spirit still lingers, seeking new goods,
And it will not hesitate to take your life,
If you dare to venture into its domain of strife.

A Flame that Never Died

Once upon a time in a land far away,
There lived two lovers, so bright and gay,
Their story was one of joy and fun,
A tale of love, that had just begun.

The boy's name was Adam, so kind and fair,
He had a smile that made hearts everywhere,
The girl's name was Lily, with eyes so bright,
She shone like a star, in the darkest night.

One day, as fate would have it,
Adam and Lily met, in a crowded street,
Their eyes met, and their hearts skipped a beat,
And they knew, this love they would not regret.

As they walked and talked, in the bright sunshine,
Their love grew stronger, with each passing time,
They laughed and joked, and had so much fun,
And they knew, that their love had just begun.

They went on dates, to parks and cafes,
They explored the city, in so many ways,
They danced and sang, and played in the rain,
Their love was a fire, that nothing could restrain.

As time went by, their love only grew,
They knew that they were meant to be true,
Their love was like a flower, that never wilted,
It only bloomed, with each day that was gifted.

One day, Adam got down on one knee,
And asked Lily, "will you marry me?",
Lily's heart skipped a beat, as she replied "yes",
And they sealed their love, with a sweet caress.

They planned their wedding, with so much love,
It was going to be a day, like none above,
Their family and friends, all gathered there,
To witness the love, that they had to share.

The wedding was beautiful, with flowers and light,
And Adam and Lily, were a stunning sight,
As they said their vows, and exchanged their rings,
Their love was a song, that the universe sings.

Years went by, and their love grew stronger,
It was a love, that could not be any longer,
They had children, who grew up so fast,
Their love was a bond, that would always last.

As they sat on their porch, in the evening light,
Adam looked at Lily, and said "you're still my delight",
Lily smiled, and replied "I love you more",
Their love was a flame, that nothing could bore.

Their love story, was one of joy and fun,
A tale of love, that had just begun,
Their love was a fire, that never died,
And their love was a song, that never lied.

And as the sun set, on their happy note,
Their love was a flame, that never would gloat,
For they knew, that their love would always be,
A love that was pure, and so full of glee.

Love Beyond Romance

In his younger years, just a teenage boy,
He longed for love, to be someone's joy.
At sixteen, a girl proposed to him,
And he was overjoyed, his heart brimmed.

But as time passed, mistakes were made,
Misunderstandings arose, the love did fade.
He thought he'd found love in another friend,
But the rejection caused their bond to end.

Two years went by, and the boy's hopes were slim,
Until he met a girl who showed him love within.
He was scared to repeat the past, to make a mistake,
So, he kept his distance, though his heart still ached.

The girl showed him what he'd never known,
That love can come from a friend, a love all its own.
They ate lunch together, studied side by side,
And their bond grew stronger, an unbreakable tie.

They conducted events, had fun and laughter,
She was always there for him, before and after.
Their friendship was priceless, the bond so strong,
It was what he'd been searching for all along.

The boy realized he didn't need a girlfriend to be happy,
For he had a friend who was always there, never snappy.
Their bond was unconditional, their love pure,
Their friendship a blessing, that would always endure.

Through thick and thin, they stood by each other,
Supporting and loving, like no other.
The boy knew he had found a friend for life,
And he was grateful to have her by his side.

He made a promise to himself that day,
To never let their friendship, fade away.
He would always be there for her, no matter what,
Their bond forever unbreakable, a precious cut.

For true love comes in many forms,
Not just romantic, but in friendships warm.
And the boy knew that he was truly blessed,
To have found a friend, who gave him her best.

So, he held on tight to the bond they'd formed,
And through the years, their love only adorned.
Their friendship remained strong,
a bond that would never break,
A promise to always be there, no matter what was at stake.